How to
encourage
Your Willing
Customers to
Come Forward and
sell for you!

By - Krishna Mohan Avancha

- The Guide To selling through organic reviews

Index:

Table of Contents

Introduction

What you do and make on your end is just 50% of the condition for your online noteworthy. The other half originates from how the customer rates & cooperates with your business and the encounters they share thus. With the ascent of web based life locales, online registries, and other moment sharing applications, online surveys have turned out to be to a great degree compelling. The short response to the topic of whether online audits matter is yes. Pursue on to get a more inside and out take a guess at why online surveys matter and exactly the amount they matter to the accomplishment of your business.

Audits Influence Buyer Behavior

Online client audits are generally utilized by customers to settle on acquiring choices.

- 90% are pursuing multiple surveys, and 15% actively are pursuing 11 audits or more)

- 88% trust online audits while thinking about a business

- 72% state that positive surveys make them trust a nearby business more

- Clients are probably going to burn through 31% more on a business with brilliant audits

- 86% of buyers will rule against purchasing from you on the off chance that they read negative audits about you on the web.

Audits Affect Your Business' Appearance in Search Results

Audits about your business don't simply affect the individuals who are searching out data about your business explicitly on the web. Keep in mind, purchasers don't generally know to look for your business explicitly. Truth be told, all things considered, a large number of your clients found your business by leading an online scan for the kind of item or administration you give, or notwithstanding for data they were looking for that is identified with your industry.

Hunt is an amazing asset today, regardless of whether on Google, Yelp, Google Maps, or somewhere else, and your appearance in query items matters—which is additionally why online surveys matter. The nearness (or need) of audits on your business specifically impacts the manner in which your business shows up in more extensive list items. Neighborhood results for Google looks, Google Maps results, and Yelp are only three instances of survey stages that demonstrate both a star rating and even a piece of the audit in their list items.

Audit Sites Matter with SEO

The more positive audits you get inside explicit catalogs, the higher your rank will be on that index and the better your business will look. In any case, did you additionally realize that a higher position or higher volume of surveys in explicit catalogs can likewise enhance your position on the index? (Google, that is). Destinations like Yelp and Angie's rundown have solid SEO, so regardless of whether your business doesn't rank on the primary page of Google for a specific inquiry, your posting on one of these indexes, or your name as a major aspect of a "Main 10 handymen in Boston" could.

This is the reason it is imperative to ensure you are reliably gathering positive audits for your business—to enable you to rank in indexed lists and furthermore to guarantee that what clients do find in results is engaging.

Surveys Have Many Marketing Benefits

Online surveys matter since they inspire more individuals to see your business. All the more essentially, they inspire a greater amount of the ideal individuals to see your business (those looking for data on it or for your items and administration), and they present your business in a positive and reliable light. (Indeed, even a negative audit, when reacted to fittingly, can indicate straightforwardness for your business). However the advantages of online audits don't stop there. Peruse on for significantly more:

Social Proof: You can compose first rate content about how extraordinary your business is, yet nothing is more valid than the endorsement of a genuine client.

Promoting Content: Reviews make for simple and powerful substance to share on your site or crosswise over social channels.

All encompassing Viewpoint: Customer surveys offer knowledge into your particular item or administrations as well as into what the general involvement of connecting with your business resembles.

Set Yourself Apart: Customers are bound to compose a survey on our business in the event that it emerged to them here and there, regularly referencing things you might not have seen yourself or thought to feature to potential clients. Saddle these little perceptions to separate yourself from contenders.

Reinforce Your Brand Identity: How you react to an audit has the same amount of an effect as the survey itself, regardless of whether that audit is certain or negative. Online surveys are chances to demonstrate your image identity and uprightness to the general population.

Assemble Trust: No business is impeccable and buyers esteem straightforwardness, so a sound blend of positive and negative surveys, joined by the best possible reactions on your end will gain you the trust of your group of onlookers

Enhance Rankings: We previously referenced this, however it merits referencing once more. Having positive online surveys can support your position and immovability on exceedingly dealt stages, for example, Google and Yelp

In addition to the fact that consumers read surveys, they read numerous audits and straightforwardly permit the nature of a business' audits to impact their trust in and commitment with that business.

Setting your business up in catalogs to get surveys and proactively connecting for audits is critical to the development of your business. Audits matter, and in the event that they're not a priority in your promoting plan, it's a great opportunity to make them one!

Why should your focus be on organic reviews

"Elective realities," "counterfeit news," these are phrases that overwhelmed media waves all through the latest decision cycle. Take a gander at your Facebook, Twitter, or any online networking outlet and you will locate your computerized world is loaded up with a downpour of misleading content, flawed stories, fake sources, fudged numbers, and straight up falsehoods.

Significantly all the more disappointing, it appears that everybody, from your uncle to that companion from secondary school you haven't conversed with in 10 years, is sharing it.

How Does This Affect Your Customers?

This atmosphere has driven buyers to be careful about most all that they read web based, including anything about your organization. As per Edelman's 2018 Trust Barometer, trust in government, business, and media has tumbled to record lows no matter how you look at it. At the end of the day, customers are less disposed to inside and out trust the guarantees brands and advertisers make to them.

While putting resources into advertisements and ads stays essential, you require something to back them up with social evidence so they don't fall upon doubtful ears.

85% of web clients state they assess a story's source before sharing it to their own profile. On the off chance that individuals are that watchful with regards to simply sending a story, you better trust they are doing their exploration with regards to acquiring choices.

In Reviews We Trust

The spine your computerized advertising needs is client audits, a vital component of trust promoting.

The world can be an alarming and dubious place, particularly in the period of phony news. Luckily, notwithstanding this, people have held some trust in different people.

Credible client surveys give associations and their items a human touch.

Actually, 85% of Millennials state surveys impact their obtaining decisions, and that is just a single statistic! Besides, over 80% of clients see client surveys with as much trust as they would an individual suggestion.

The most effective method to Get Started with Customer Reviews

Getting Reviewed

In the event that this numerous individuals are dissecting surveys amid their purchaser's adventure, it is fundamental that you figure out how to utilize them adequately.

The initial step is to enlist your business on outsider audit destinations, for example,

- Cry
- Google Local
- Angie's List
- TrustPilot
- Foursquare.

You can even investigate industry-explicit locales that share audits.

The way to producing a higher number of positive surveys is to make the audit procedure as clear as could reasonably be expected.

Ensure that connects to these locales are obviously set on your business' site. You can even have a go at catching up with clients through email, urging them to impart their positive experience to your organization or item. Their purchasing knowledge will in any case be new in their psyches now, prompting a progressively precise survey.

Whenever left unprompted, buyers are bound to make a special effort to leave a survey simply after a negative ordeal. At long last, looking for criticism can even show you some things about how to enhance your very own business.

Additionally, connect with clients via web-based networking media, gatherings, and audit locales. Pay additional consideration to existing clients, urge them to give input, and you will wind up with your very own grassroots promoting group that will proselytize steadfastness to your image.

Dealing with Your Customer Reviews

While actualizing your new client audit system, make sure to never deliver counterfeit surveys. Counterfeit audits are the human sin of the computerized network.

In addition to the fact that they are phony audits exploitative, clients can more often than not spot them from a mile away and they can accomplish more harm than a bone-fide awful survey.

In the event that you do locate a negative audit staring you in the face, don't freeze. Negative surveys are not the apocalypse. Indeed, they are superior to no surveys by any stretch of the imagination.

As Peter Muhlmann of AdWeek stated, "Reacting freely to the individuals who have had an antagonistic involvement with the brand resembles winning the promoting lottery in the period of doubt." It allows you to draw in with your clients in an individual and legit way and whenever done all around ok, you may even purpose the issue and recover the buyer's reliability.

How Customer Reviews Impact Sales

Buyer's adoring your image is extraordinary and all, however how can it relate back to deals? The short answer is - the more clients you fulfill, the more that will need to purchase your item - however this is a misrepresented clarification of the reiteration of ways that client surveys impact your business' computerized nearness and thus, deals.

Audits not just show buyers that your image is dependable, they likewise can possibly exponentially enhance your business' SEO.

Web indexes might be fueled by coding and calculations, however they have figured out how to fuse a human viewpoint also. Client surveys (particularly positive ones on Google Pages) are social confirmation that your business is authentic and valid. The outcome is a higher web search tool rank.

Client audits enable your SEO to bloom, as well as influence navigate rates. Essentially having an audit or item appraising in your page's meta portrayal can enhance navigate rates as much as 20% by bringing down rubbing and building trust before a guest even gets on the page.!

Generally speaking, client audits are a fundamental piece during the time spent persuading prospects that your item or administration is superior to the opposition and genuinely offers the esteem that you are moving.

For purchasers, it is a vote of certainty that the buy choice they're influencing will to be a decent one, and this certainty makes them all the more ready to make all necessary endorsements.

Key Takeaway

Disregarding what others think might be a word of wisdom for your own life, however with regards to your business, it should be handled head-on.

Client audits can possibly transform a un-involved customer into a deep rooted, faithful purchaser.

In a period when shoppers are doubtful of everything, client audits are held to a higher standard. We experience a daily reality such that John Doe's feeling on an item is similarly as significant as that of an industry master.

These tips can help you proactively confront the test of credibility. Put resources into trust advertising and thus, put resources into the accomplishment of your business.

Power of reviews and how it influences what we buy

Imagine a situation where you decide you want to buy a radio. The first thing you do would be either to go to your local store or go online and check the reviews there. It has become such a repetitive task that sellers these days write fake reviews to influence you to buy their product or services. Go to your local store. You might not find this type of selling there as more than wanting to sell the wish to keep the relationship going is a greater influencer. To understand this more in detail, you will need to visit at least 4-5 local stores with a simple request for them to explain what you want to buy. Our of the 4-5 stores you will notice that the 3 that you may not have visited often would end up giving you advises and also making some over the normal claims. This is the same technique that your online store tried to use with you.

The want to sell is so strong with these people that they have forgotten to add the value which you would need and try to push the product. This is also the method which goes against consumerism, or the protection or promotion of the interests of consumers. The store owners may not be bad people but now it is past them.

What is

Consumerism

The embodiment of each economy is development. In any case, the miserable part is that for monetary success and competency, nations around the globe have ignored ecological preservation and well-being. Commercialization, which has developed at an extraordinary pace, got with it piles of waste and no payment for our oversights.

As indicated by World Bank, as of now, 1.3 billion tons of city strong waste is produced on the planet and this is relied upon to increment to 2.2 billion tons by 2025. Studies have appeared higher pay levels and expanded urbanization mean squander is created on the grounds that use levels increment with ascend in expendable wages.

A standout amongst the most hurtful waste being created in wealth is plastic. Since the progressive innovation of plastic during the 1950s, the buyer showcase changed. Plastics, being made at a fast rate, have immersed our presence since it is shoddy, sturdy, and lightweight. That is the manner by which it turned into a key component in business tasks, for example, stockpiling, transportation, development and so on. In the previous 50 years, plastic creation has expanded from 15 million tons (1964) to 311 million tons (2014), and is relied upon to twofold again throughout the following 20 years.

In the time of commercialization, helpful and simple to-utilize items have assumed control over the market and since plastic is modest and tough, single-use plastics have turned into an exceptionally ordinary. Single-use plastics, frequently additionally alluded to as dispensable plastics, are normally utilized for bundling things. These incorporate, among different things, staple sacks, nourishment bundling, bottles, straws, holders, mugs and cutlery. A World Economic Forum report expresses that starting at 2016, 95% of plastic bundling material esteem, or $80– $120 billion every year, is lost to the economy after a short first use.

The most well-known single-use plastics found in the earth are, arranged by size, cigarette butts, plastic drinking bottles, plastic jug tops, nourishment wrappers, plastic staple sacks, plastic tops, straws and stirrers, different sorts of plastic packs, and froth remove compartments.

Prior this year, the European Commission 2018 took strict measures against the main 10 single-use plastics found in the seas and oceans around them. The 10 such things on European shorelines represent 43% of total marine litter, angling gear speaks to an extra 27% of all marine litter. The commission is acting in these two regions, which speak to 70% of all marine litter found on Europe's shorelines.

Indian situation

The issue India faces is that the rate of generation of plastics, besides single-use plastics, is a lot higher than the worldwide reusing rate. Subsequently, the size of waste administration is infinitesimal when contrasted with the rate of waste age.

In spite of the fact that India's plastic waste generation isn't as vast as other created or creating countries, the country battles with overseeing and arranging this waste. India has no information on single-utilize plastic waste in light of the fact that there is no definition for such plastics here. Another explanation behind this is isolation of single-use plastics is a laborious undertaking and a lot of plastic waste is isolated and reused by the casual division. India must pursue the strides of EU in light of the fact that there is a prompt need for us to characterize our loss for it to be overseen better.

The prohibition on certain plastic items in 25 states/UTs gives trust, yet the execution so far has been below average. A sweeping boycott will neither help merchants, nor shoppers as neither of them are aware of the waste administration system to have the capacity to end plastics. This strategy intercession requires something other than enactment.

Customers frame the market's center and that is the reason the way toward wiping out single-use plastics must starts with us. The most clear and fundamental answer for this is reusing. We should move back to a culture of reusable items or options in contrast to plastics (steel, wood, mud), with the end goal that the measure of waste created is limited. Nonetheless, this requires a great deal of venture, which may not interest all segments of society. Plastics being an impressively less expensive material contrasted with other crude materials, the expense to a customer is additionally less expensive. This demonstrates creative Eco-structures must be supported.

Shoppers should likewise be urged to present cuts in utilizing plastics. A standout amongst the best types of boost is tax assessment. For instance, before declaring the assessment, in Ireland, retailers gave out 1.26 billion plastic packs each year, with a normal use of 328 sacks for each individual every year. The administration determined shoppers' readiness to pay (WTP) for plastic sacks and forced an expense many times the WTP. With the help of smooth usage and very much characterized administration capacities for various gatherings, inside one year the use of plastic packs in Ireland dropped by over 90% and the use per individual tumbled from 328 plastic sacks for every year to 21 sacks. Moreover, while before the 2002 need, plastic packs represented 5% of the national waste, in 2004 this number tumbled to 0.22%.

We have achieved a point where our activities have cost us and interest in ecological security is fundamental. Venture from the legislature will be supported by the income it wins, and it's time we are saddled for our conduct. The WEF Report assesses that by 2050 there will be more plastic in the sea than fish. The manner in which we have been "pushing ahead", all things considered, it won't be the fish swimming in our waste.

Why Buyers believe in reviews?

Buyers are now captivating more with online audits in 2018 than they did a year ago. They are bound to leave progressively positive surveys, and bound to anticipate that a reaction should negative audit from a business. We studied in excess of 400 customers to discover the best online audits inclines in 2018 for neighborhood organizations.

As indicated by the 2018 Review-Trackers Online Reviews Survey, 63.6 percent of shoppers state they are probably going to check online audits on Google before visiting a business — more than those counseling some other audit web-page.

In excess of 90 percent of organizations have no less than one survey on Google, while just 40 percent of organizations have audits on Facebook.

Google's prevalence implies organizations need to give careful consideration to the components that influence neighborhood look and their appearance on Google.

In excess of 35 percent of all pursuit traffic has nearby plan, as indicated by research by Review-Trackers. Neighborhood look traffic implies you must enhance your online nearness for nearby pursuit. One approach to upgrade for neighborhood seek is to deal with your business' Google My Business page.

A case of a nearby inquiry is the point at which a purchaser types "specialists in Chicago" in the hunt box on Google. Google will at that point demonstrate the customer surveys, star appraisals, and where nearby specialists are situated on the guide.

Survey signals are one of Google's main eight deciding variables that influence where a business winds up in neighborhood seek. Audit signals incorporate the measure of surveys your business has and how regularly surveys are posted.

To say it essentially: on the off chance that you get a huge amount of positive surveys, Google will demonstrate your business in more list items.

The client encounter you give disconnected is a deciding component of your image's notoriety on the web. Notwithstanding, giving a client encounter that meets or surpasses desires is simply part of what will make your notoriety emerge.

Think about that 53 percent of clients anticipate that a business should react to their online audits inside seven days. Ninety-four percent of purchasers state an online survey has persuaded them to maintain a strategic distance from a business — 94 percent.

There's uplifting news with regards to online audits patterns.

Albeit negative surveys persuade customers to keep away from a business, 45 percent of purchasers state they are bound to visit a business with negative audits if the business reacts to those surveys. While a negative audit is harming, tending to a client's grumbling can really enhance your notoriety altogether.

4. 2018 will be the time of brand notoriety (notwithstanding for private company)

Discussing on the web surveys patterns, each business is currently appraised. Scan for a business and you'll see stars recorded by their name.

It comes down to client encounter. Clients will be bound to compose a positive negative survey after a positive ordeal. At the point when the client feels like the person in question can tell different shoppers that the business is more than worth the buyer's time and cash, that is the point at which they'll boast about you on the web.

Surveys are a device to enhance the client encounter. Tune in to what clients are stating. Utilize that data to enhance the client encounter. On the off chance that clients state the fries are saturated, make them un-wet.

With online audits patterns, it doesn't make a difference whether you run a nourishment truck in Austin or a bookkeeping firm in New York — surveys will influence your business.

Be that as it may, surveys don't influence each industry similarly.

For organizations in the fund and protection businesses, a greater number of customers this year than a year ago state they are probably going to leave an audit about a positive ordeal, as per the review. Just 13 percent of purchasers said they were probably going to leave an audit after a positive involvement with a bank in 2017, contrasted with 19 percent in 2018. For protection, that number expanded from 14 percent in 2017 to 18 percent in 2018.

While these increments are something to be thankful for, how about we contrast those numbers with the eatery business. At the point when gotten some information about eateries, 43 percent of purchasers said they'd leave a positive audit after a decent ordeal — which implies that eatery visitors are 2.4 occasions bound to leave a decent survey than a shopper who visits a bank or protection specialist. That implies monetary administrations will have need to work twice as hard as eateries to get audits.

While you may feel that this implies audits are less imperative in enterprises like saving money, it's not valid. The greater part of purchasers state surveys are persuasive while picking another bank. What's more, in excess of 60 percent of customers state audits are compelling while picking a protection specialist. Customers still search for surveys in these enterprises — regardless of whether they're more averse to abandon them.

The takeaway for an entrepreneur: Your industry may give difficulties to you with regards to getting more surveys and keeping up a high star rating.

Your most amazing weapon for social verification

Audit the board is just expanding in significance for your image notoriety. It's urgent that you produce audits, react to surveys, and deal with your nearby postings, particularly Google My Business.

Online surveys are the apparatuses shoppers use to settle on choices about where to take their business. As our information demonstrates us, customers are just going to be progressively connected with audits in 2018. It'll be up to ensure they're tuning in to their clients on the web. They'll have to react to any issues that surface in surveys to make the experience charming for all clients.

8 ways you could use the customer reviews in your day-day marketing activities

The most ideal approach to manufacture your validity as a business (notwithstanding giving uncommon items and administrations, obviously) is to fabricate a positive notoriety through your dealings with clients. Be that as it may, other than verbal, how would you share all the extraordinary things existing clients are stating about your business to reign in new crowds? Here are eight different ways you can utilize client surveys in your computerized advertising to help your believability and contact more individuals.

1. Show Them on the Homepage of Your Website

Notwithstanding having an assigned page for tributes, you ought to likewise make the best surveys noticeable on each and every page of your site. Maybe one distinctive tribute for each page. That way, guests are continually reminded in a little, non-meddling way that others hold your business in such high regard.

2. Use Them in Marketing Collateral

Join your best client audits in your handouts, move sheets, and other advertising insurance when you share data about your business with new potential clients. As per Social Media Today, 88 percent of customers trust online surveys in indistinguishable respect from individual proposals. Surveys give your current business data that additional push of believability.

3. Incorporate Them in Your Pricing Packages

To legitimize the expense of your items or administrations, show client audits inside your estimating bundles. This will enable potential clients to see the estimation of your business and think of it as worth the venture.

4. Place Them on Your Business Cards

Counting only one best survey on your business cards will establish a long term connection that will reach data for your business even more worth having.

5. Feature Them in Your Promotional Videos

Incorporate an area for client audits or disperse them all through any special recordings for your business. While clients are watching to take in more about your business, surveys fill in as an unpretentious update that you've fulfilled other individuals.

6. Incorporate Them in Your Email Communication

Pick your most loved client survey and add it to your email signature. Likewise, maybe incorporate an alternate client survey toward the finish of each mass email you disseminate to clients on your email rundown to give that little update that your business is the best which is as it should be.

7. Grandstand Them on Your Blog

On the off chance that you have a different website for your business' blog, figure out how to grandstand your most loved audits on the fundamental page to expand guests' confidence in your skill on the points you're blogging about.

8. Offer Them on Social Media

This is maybe the most critical of all the approaches to share client audits to help validity. Buyers will in general swing to web-based social networking to decide if a business is valid. Notwithstanding taking a gander at the quantity of devotees or preferences your page or record has, they likewise take a gander at your surveys and appraisals. Ensure your audits are effectively perceptible on the majority of your web based life profiles—t can have an enormous effect.

6 Ways to Grow Customer Reviews

For a few, surveys can be unnerving, on account of the likelihood of getting scornful, negative audits that dirt your image's picture. In any case, as an entrepreneur, you require surveys in light of the fact that they bring more great than mischief (even negative audits are useful for your business, trust it or not, but rather more on that later). Surveys work as an advanced informal, as tributes that can shape how new page guests see your business. Truth be told, surveys convey validity to your business. As per Vendasta Technologies, a Canadian PC programming organization, 80% of clients trust surveys as much as they trust individual suggestions.

So now you most likely need to develop your client audits as fast as could reasonably be expected. Here are six powerful ways you can do that.

1. Give Feedback First

For this situation, the proverb "the timely riser gets the worm" seems to be valid. In the event that you give positive input first, your beneficiaries will feel more constrained to give back where its due. Regular obligingness (if the beneficiaries have any) will propel them to do as such. This strategy functions admirably for organizations that work with web based business sites or applications that permit both the merchant and the client to rate each other, sites and applications, for example, eBay, Amazon, and Uber.

When you've given positive criticism, approach your client for an audit by means of private message. You can hold up a couple of days in the wake of leaving your criticism to do this to guarantee that they see your audit first. (Most sites and applications advise its clients when they get criticism.)

2. Request the Review

Some of the time when you ask, you will get. This is valid for surveys. In the event that you need an audit, don't be hesitant to inquire. All things considered, the more regrettable reaction you'll get is a no (on the off chance that you'll get a reaction by any means). When you ask, ask by means of private message. This can be through an informing highlight of an outsider web-page you use or an email in case you're moving through your own site. Straightforwardly requesting an audit, or putting clients under the spotlight, will probably constrain them to react. Have you ever request some help in a gathering visit and got no reaction? Have you attempted specifically informing one of the beneficiaries from the gathering talk and got a reaction? Asking straightforwardly and graciously works.

3. Request a Review at the Right Time

When you request an audit, make a point to ask at the perfect time. For instance, in case you're engaged with internet business, it is absurd to request an audit before your client has gotten your item. Keep in mind that your purchaser will probably get your item inside no less than seven days—enough time for your purchaser to disregard your demand. Or maybe, request an audit one to two days after your client has gotten your item. (Following reveals to you when the item has arrived.)

4. Give Incentives

On the off chance that specifically requesting audits doesn't work, have a go at giving motivations. For instance, you can offer limits, coupon codes, or free transporting in return for audits. When you do this, be that as it may, ensure that you give your offer a period limit to empower snappy activity.

5. Embed CTAs in Your Website

Numerous online life gadgets and modules that let you embed a CTA on your site exist. Utilize these to urge web guests to leave an audit about your business. Remark Rating Field, Author Review, Rich Reviews, and WP Review are simple ones to utilize. On the off chance that you have a Facebook page, you can structure a CTA that urges guests to leave an audit on your Facebook page. You can do likewise for different web based life pages, for example, Yelp, Google, and Angie's List.

6. Development

On the off chance that you specifically informed a client for an audit and didn't get a reaction, attempt once more. Hang tight for possibly 14 days before you development, and just follow up once. You would prefer not to sound malicious, all things considered. Also, when you development, dependably do as such obligingly. Try not to sound excessively pushy.

In the event that you need to develop your client surveys, recollect that you can do as such utilizing a few or the majority of the six strategies recorded above: you can leave an audit first, request a survey, request an audit at the correct time, give motivating forces, embed CTAs in your site, or development. Audits, great or awful, are useful to your business, so don't give terrible surveys a chance to alarm you.

Truth be told, it's smarter to keep awful audits than to erase them, a demonstration which may cause some doubt. Keeping terrible surveys demonstrates straightforwardness and develops trust from your clients. As opposed to erasing terrible audits, react to them. It demonstrates that you're willing to take care of issues and cooperate with your clients.

Who is a consumer and what are there types?

Shoppers are the fundamental financial substances of an economy. Every one of the buyers devour merchandise and ventures specifically and in a roundabout way to augment fulfillment and utility.

Shoppers have constrained salary and by which they need to fulfill their greatest (utility is the need fulfilling limit of a ware).

By and large, buyer implies an individual just; be that as it may, buyers will comprise of a specific individual, a gathering of people, foundations and so on.

As indicated by the idea of utilization, customers are of following sorts:

(I) Direct Consumers:

History discloses to us that at the beginning time of civilization makers created all the fundamental needs of life for themselves and their families. All the fundamental needs like sustenance, apparel and safe house they created for their own and their family's utilization. Thus, the makers were creating merchandise for their self-utilization. In this way, they were called as immediate shoppers or direct makers moreover.

(ii) Consumers by Exchanging Products:

With entry of time and civilization individuals comprehended the advantages of trade. Henceforth, they attempted to practice on a specific or couple of items and afterward endeavored to trade the item with alternate product(s). The trade began with deal framework and now proceeding with money related framework.

This will make the idea of attractive overflow, i.e., the makers are creating merchandise for self-utilization, as well as some overabundance or surplus product(s) they are keeping to get different product(s) in return. For instance, an agriculturist creating beat for self-utilization as well as the additional or surplus heartbeat he will trade with the maker of other item, state paddy.

(iii) Modern Consumers:

These customers just go to the market to purchase the merchandise and ventures accessible in the market through cash as it were. Here, the makers are likewise creating merchandise or administrations specifically sent to the market for the shoppers. These customers purchase every one of the products and ventures in lieu of cash. The advanced shoppers are the result of money related framework.

(Significance) of Consumers:

The significance of customers in various roads is talked about underneath:

(I) Encourage Demand:

Customers are the principle wellspring of interest for every one of the merchandise. The makers of mechanical merchandise or the makers of farming items are on the whole creating the different things as indicated by the interest in the market. As per Prof. Marshall, it is the interest which controls the generation or market. Henceforth, the shoppers make request in the market and makers deliver products or administrations as needs be.

(ii) Create Demand for Various Products:

The diverse buyers have distinctive kinds of interest or a solitary purchaser can likewise request diverse sorts of items. These will urge the makers to create different sorts of items in the market. For instance, a few shoppers need to devour paddy, though a few customers need to expend wheat.

Be that as it may, there are a few customers; who need diverse characteristics of paddy and wheat too. Along these lines, there are a few purchasers who lean toward red shading cleanser though other' buyers favor green shading cleanser. Accordingly, to fulfill every one of the kinds of customers, makers must build the creation of different items.

(iii) Increase Demand for Consumer Goods:

Purchasers make more interest for every one of the sorts of buyer merchandise, as strong, semi-tough and transient products. Sturdy buyer merchandise incorporate furnishings, utensils, TVs, and so forth and for semi-strong products like garments, books, shoes and so on. Then again, transient merchandise like bread, margarine, vegetables, organic products and so forth are altogether requested by the buyers for their utilization purposes. Normally, all these make a climate to build interest for shopper products.

(iv) Enhance Service Diversification:

Shoppers devour distinctive assortments of products, as well as expend extensive assortments of administrations to keep up the way of life. These incorporate wellbeing administration, instructive administration, managing an account and protection administration, transport and correspondence benefit, and so forth. Step by step the utilization of these administrations is rising. This will prompt development or improvement of administration segment inside the economy.

13 Free User Feedback Tools for Digital Marketers on a Budget

Client input is the key pointer of client encounter. Approaching the client bits of knowledge puts you as an advertiser at an upper hand. Truth be told, client criticism will likewise empower you to organize and address issues that surface, putting you one bit nearer to achieving a beneficial end and shutting the circle. That is the reason it's critical to have the correct client input arrangement set up, contingent upon your requirements and obviously, spending plan. In this article we will focus in on a few free client input instruments that are extraordinary for advanced advertisers who are on a financial plan.

Remember that client input devices can be extremely various in purpose.They frequently utilize an assortment of gathering methods, gather distinctive types of criticism, report contrastingly and give various types of bits of knowledge to the client. To illuminate, here is a breakdown of the client criticism classifications highlighted in this post.

Free Voice of Customer Tools

Regardless of whether you're a startup hoping to minimize expenses, an advanced advertiser who's having questions about which apparatus to utilize, or only a plain old scrooge, we have a lot of free client input instruments for you to look over. How about we investigate.

Free Voice of Customer (VoC) Tools

Voice of the Customer (VoC) apparatuses are turning into a #1 need among online organizations – for the most part in light of the fact that these sorts of devices have turned into a basic component in client encounter activities. VoC instruments make it simple for guests to convey about their client encounter specifically and abstain from interfering with the online voyage. They are likewise extraordinary for gathering 'in-the-occasion' (or continuous) criticism.

1. Feedbackify

With Feedbackify you can make input shapes all without anyone else, in addition to establishment is simple (reordering the code into your site's HTML). Your guests can give a rating and additionally submit remarks, including proposals and compliments. You can likewise see all criticism got in a dashboard continuously including sifting by class and sub-classification.

Site: www.feedbackify.com

2. UserReport

UserReport is a VoC apparatus that gathers input in two diverse ways: by means of an overview or their criticism discussion. The criticism review works a ton like Feedbackify, yet additionally offers Net Promoter Score (NPS) as a measurement. The criticism discussion, or network, enables clients to gather thoughts and channel by well known, latest, and shut thoughts. Your guests can post, vote on and talk about these thoughts in the network.

Site: www.userreport.com

3. Omniconvert

While Omniconvert might be increasingly centered around boosting changes utilizing A/B testing, it is additionally an incredible (and free!) instrument for conveying VoC studies. This device rearranges how you work together by taking the outcomes from these studies and transforming them into significant experiences and thoughts. Omniconvert likewise incorporates various personalisation alternatives with the goal that you can make customized messages and show them to your group of onlookers.

Site: www.omniconvert.com

Free Online Review Tools

Online Review Tools are a perfect device in the event that you need to develop trust among your guests on the web. Utilized habitually by advanced advertisers in light of the notable Google Stars, these apparatuses can positively affect Google Rankings. Survey instruments can likewise impact acquiring conduct seeing as how the greater part of clients see audits before buying an item or administration. In any case, remember that all surveys (positive or negative) are shared openly with your guests...

4. Howl

Howl is an extremely outstanding web audit and rating site that is made for neighborhood organizations and eateries. The apparatus utilizes long-frame surveys to get point by point reactions from analysts. All your business needs to do is initiate a Yelp business page. To help the quantity of surveys you get, you can likewise add an identification to your site that demands audits, or convey a connection in your organization bulletins. Also, truth is stranger than fiction! Howl offers a free suite of instruments that enable you to react to the audits and track guest commitment.

Site: www.yelp.com

5. Trustspot.io

TrustSpot underpins organization surveys, item audits, or both! With this apparatus, clients can make a profile page and make gadgets for their site to gather surveys. TrustSpot likewise gives an incorporated examination usefulness that gives clients knowledge into how clients are drawing in with messages (audit demands). This instrument offers standard reconciliations with different webshop frameworks, for example, Shopify and Magento.

Site: www.trustpost.com

6. Yotpo

Yotpo positions itself as a client content promoting stage, which arrangements, for example, visual showcasing, shopper bits of knowledge and obviously, surveys and evaluations. This device enables you to change over 10% of your clients into analysts! Email your clients, at a set time after buy and urge them to leave surveys for items they've obtained. You can likewise put Yotpo's customisable gadgets wherever you need individually site. These gadgets incorporates a trustbadge, inside and out data about the commentator, and they enable you to ask your purchasers addresses that may enable them to settle on a choice.

Site: www.yotpo.com

Free Online Survey Tools

Maybe a standout amongst the most mainstream kinds of apparatuses are online review instruments. Frequently as an input catch or email welcome, these apparatuses have turned out to be very well known since the rise of site criticism. A portion of these apparatuses are centered around specific specialties while others focus on client encounter. Before, these input instruments were outstanding for their propensity to incorporate a considerable rundown of inquiries, anyway these days, they are getting to be shorter and shorter – which surely makes them to a lesser extent a problem for respondents.

Interestingly, a considerable lot of these apparatuses haven't a lot to offer as far as inside and out investigation.

7. Zoho Survey

Zoho Survey gives their customers a wide choice of inherent reports and intuitive diagrams to enable them to break down and understand the overview results and infer astute, noteworthy bits of knowledge. Since Zoho Survey bolsters numerous dialects, you can make overviews meant in excess of 30 dialects. Reviews can be shared via web-based networking media channels, inserted on your site or opened utilizing a QR code. This instrument is incredible for organizations who need to coordinate their study device with a CRM (for example Zoho CRM).

Site: www.zoho.com

8. PollDaddy

With this free client criticism arrangement, clients can make, disperse, and decipher the consequences of surveys, reviews, tests and appraisals. Clients can insert these overviews on their site rapidly and effectively or welcome respondents by means of email. When the information is gathered, you can make channels to break down the information and offer it in reports. The aftereffects of these overviews would all be able to be seen continuously. The free bundle, be that as it may, just offers space for one client, there are no fare choices and you can't tweak the look-and-feel of your reviews.

Site: www.polldaddy.com

9. Study Monkey

Study Monkey is a well known client criticism answer for making overviews. Its free form gives you boundless studies yet limits you to 10 questions for every review. Furthermore, it's anything but difficult to-utilize UI makes it simple to request contribution from your clients, clients, and representatives. This apparatus is ideal for erratic studies, anyway this makes it less appropriate as far as estimating in general fulfillment or re-studying clients again after a specific timeframe.

Site: www.surveymonkey.com

10. Google Forms

Google Forms is one more free online study programming that enables its clients to rapidly and effectively assembled overviews by means of a drag and drop interface. As far as plan, these studies can be altogether modified. The instrument furnishes you with ongoing reaction information and graphs. This information can likewise be associated with other Google items.

Site: www.google.com

Free Visual Feedback Tools

On the off chance that you are progressively keen on catching client contribution on specific site page components, at that point maybe a visual criticism apparatus is something worth considering. Some give the alternative present a screen capture while others make utilization of virtual sticky notes that feature certain components on the page (for example content, pictures or catches). Remember, while these give a great deal of help as far as plan they are fairly fundamental as far as extricating profound client encounter bits of knowledge.

11. Mopin.io

Mopin.io is a free visual input apparatus that empowers its clients to lead client testing on new points of arrival and additionally web architectures. This client input arrangement does not require any establishment. All input is gathered utilizing a produced, abbreviated URL of the site page you need to get criticism on. You will get input in your inbox. There is likewise the alternative to incorporate with the Mopinion Suite (paid programming). NOTE: mopin.io is produced by input programming pro Mopinion.

The immortality potion that reviews give

Customer reviews are usually seen as a unbiased and unhampered statement of a person telling why a certain product or a service is good or bad. It is equivalent to having a person standing outside your store and telling the people whether going in your store is worth their time or not. You may never need to give any discounts or offers post good reviews as the more people read them, the more they will come seeking your product or service.

People seek other people suggestion so as to not fall prey to some gimmick or lose money to some person's plot. So a honest feedback however short or sweet it may be goes a long way in establishing a brand and making the product or service a huge hit. So the happy customer you may have ignored may be the only marketing gimmick you may have ever to endure to make your product or service last forever! If you think the shell life of your product or service is about to end then try getting in a few positive honest reviews and see how easily the shell life of your product or service would extend to another decade or so.

The idea here is to get organic reviews through incentive based technique so as to establish a win-win situation with your customer and give them a sense of control. This way your customer will not just seek your product out but also tell their friends, family and people around about your wonderful product/service.

Matthew McNaughton had once quoted famously about reading a review," There's a gap between what I want to do, what I do on camera, and what gets edited. Right? So the goal is to try and close the gaps. What's the biggest compliment is if I read a review and it's exactly what I wrote down in my diary before ever filming it. That's really cool. That's the biggest signifier of closing the gaps."

Reaching the tipping point with reviews

The tipping point is a standout amongst the most wanted focuses to hit for any blogger. The tipping point speaks to a goliath flood of traffic that increments past desires. It is the sort of traffic that takes a blog from a couple of hundred guests consistently to a large number of day by day guests in a generally brief timeframe.

At the point when my blog hit its tipping point, it initially got 500 perspectives consistently. At that point, step by step, my viewership multiplied until the point that this blog got to 25,000 month to month sees. It just took a couple of months to make that huge change. While this change was occurring, I was using numerous devices and assets to develop my essence, however I didn't know everything that I know now. So as to make your blog hit a tipping point, these are the six things you have to concentrate on:

#1: Provide Valuable Content

Advancing your substance just goes up until now. One thing that decides your prosperity as a blogger is what number of individuals advance your substance. Scarcely any individuals are fit for influencing substance to become famous online all alone. Just the Oprah types can achieve such an accomplishment. 99% of the time, content becomes a web sensation when the general population in your gathering of people share that content with their companions, and those companions share the substance with their companions. Rehash the procedure multiple times with every companion, and after that you have viral substance.

In any case, individuals are not going to discuss your substance since it is there. Individuals basically talk about incredibly poor or profitable substance. The poor substance gets slammed while the important substance gets applauded. Profitable substance is the substance that successes on the web and gets shared the most. Important substance results in all the more returning guests and more grounded connections among you and your perusers. Try not to be hesitant to give free an incentive on your blog. By and large, it is the free esteem that supports the deal. So you'll profit at any rate.

#2: Grow Your Email List

You need to hear me out on this one. I began concentrating on my email list a couple of years subsequent to making this blog. That was by a long shot, undoubtably, without inquiry the greatest mix-up I made with this blog (I'm accentuating this which is as it should be). Out of the initial 100,000 guests who visited this blog, I didn't get 300 endorsers in light of the fact that my blog was inadequately upgraded to get more supporters. Your email list is so essential since it gives you a simple method to speak with your endorsers, and the navigate rates are unimaginable. Regardless of whether you just get a 5% navigate for your messages, that is an a lot higher measurement than the level of snap throughs you would get via web-based networking media (quite often under 1%).

A few advertisers go as far to state that the span of your email list demonstrates your pay. A large portion of the effective bloggers who influence six figure livelihoods to have more than 10,000 endorsers (despite the fact that having 10,000 supporters does not ensure a six figure salary, having that numerous supporters is exceptionally useful). These web journals get a flood in rush hour gridlock when an email impact gets sent to endorsers advancing the most recent article. Envision having a rundown of 10,000 email locations, and 7% of those individuals tapped on the connection. That is an additional 700 guests just from that one email. A portion of those guests may choose to share the blog entry via web-based networking media (extremely accommodating for SEO) or compose a blog entry about your blog entry. The greater part of the blog entries that I advance on this blog (aren't mine) are blog entries composed by Seth Godin. I've been perusing his messages each day for more than two years. That is not an occurrence. I normally share connects to blog entries that I read in my inbox first.

Try not to commit a similar error I made. Construct your email list now. It is your main need for transforming blogging into a full-time pay.

#3: Grow Your Social Media Audience

When you compose significant substance and have points of arrival set up to gather email addresses, those pages require perceivability. The web is an uproarious place with a huge number of sites. Somebody finding your blog (or anybody's blog so far as that is concerned) resembles finding the needle in the sheaf. A few needles in the bundle get discovered more regularly than others. All together for your needle (blog) to be found in the bundle (the web) all the more regularly, you have to advance your substance via web-based networking media.

Not exclusively is building your web based life crowd an extraordinary method to advance your substance, however it is fundamental towards setting up your power on the web.

Having a vast online life group of onlookers gives you better social verification. Consider it along these lines. Okay rather purchase the Twitter control from the individual with 100 devotees or the individual with 100,000 adherents? Would you rather take the Facebook course from the coach with 1,000 Facebook likes or the mentor with 1 million Facebook likes. When you develop your online life group of onlookers, you can utilize the social verification to support your believability.

Regardless of what you do, never resort to purchasing counterfeit adherents. In addition to the fact that it hurts your believability, the phony devotees will never draw in with you. They will likewise make your genuine devotees feel awkward. Here is an intriguing contextual investigation from Social Media Today about somebody who purchased 50,000 Twitter supporters (and was nauseated by the outcomes).

#4: Boost Your Blog's SEO

To numerous bloggers, SEO is as yet confounding. The principle reason SEO appears to be befuddling is on the grounds that there are such a large number of components that go into a web search tool's positioning framework. Some web index strategies, for example, including alt labels don't really enhance the estimation of your blog entries. Those kinds of web index enhancements are the ones that complete off camera so web crawlers can comprehend what your blog is about.

My suggestion is to just gain proficiency with a couple SEO strategies at once and actualize them one by one. Concentrate on enhancing your blog's skip rate, connecting to your other blog entries, incorporating alt labels in your photos, developing your web based life group of onlookers (that assists with SEO) and composing longer blog entries (while keeping the esteem). My proposal is to ace one of these tips at once and after that proceed onward to another arrangement of tips. You can begin with any five hints you want. I composed a blog entry that contains a couple of more tips about boosting your blog's SEO.

#5: Put In More Work Than You Already Are

On the off chance that you need to make it to the following dimension in anything, you need to put in the following dimension of work. The additional time you focus on blogging, the more remote you will go. On the off chance that you invest twice as much energy examining diverse strategies you can use to help SEO, get more supporters, and develop your online networking crowd, at that point you will have twice as much information in those regions. On the off chance that you invest twice as much energy composing content, that substance will most likely be longer and progressively significant.

It is conceivable to achieve a tipping point for your blog, however achieving that tipping point (or anything essential and worth the time) isn't a simple undertaking. I composed blog entries consistently notwithstanding when I realized nobody would see them. It was the way toward composing each day that enabled me to improve, adapt new traps, and transform my blog into what it is today.

#6: Persistence

A blogger's adventure is one of constancy. For the normal blogger, it takes a couple of years before his endeavors transform into a full-time salary. Each blogger, even the best ones, began without any crowds of their own. Effective bloggers needed to battle their way through the commotion as they developed their email records and web based life crowds. It takes a very long time of research to ace SEO and half a month of research to realize what happens when Google turns out with a noteworthy web index refresh.

In the event that you are persevering, and you adapt new methods en route, you will end up being a fruitful blogger. Be understanding, keep on putting in the work, and achievement will welcome you on the opposite side.

In Conclusion

Tipping point focus takes a ton of work to pull off, yet any business can encounter a tipping point, the minute when Sales takes off like never before previously. Indeed, even the best sales person encounters tipping focuses in their internet based life groups of onlookers, reviews, and the quantity of supporters they get.

How to build a popular review blog?

On the off chance that you construct a decent blog in the end you will appreciate the chance to survey items and administrations that can produce income through direct deals or partner advancements. The secret to make this gainful without driving off your pursuers, is to compose a thorough, fair audit that still believers easygoing pursuers into purchasers, who make a move that profits income for you.

Publicizing versus Audits

Before we hop into how to compose a survey that moves, I trust it is imperative to illuminate the contrast between ordinary promoting and an audit. Both of these mediums are types of media introduction that have the objective of persuading an individual to play out an activity, however at their center... they are altogether different.

Regular Advertising – Advertising is frequently only a speedy pitch that keeps that explicit brand name in your mind sufficiently long for you to play out an activity (normally a buy). The promotion is set up by a showcasing firm or the organization creating the item and it includes just the perspectives the organization needs to depict. Ads are regularly tossed through numerous sessions of statistical surveying and are vigorously adapted towards the brain research of the intended interest group.

Surveys – When done accurately, audits are a far reaching take a gander at the great and terrible of an item or administration as it identifies with its intended interest group. A commentator isn't associated with the host organization to avert inclination in the auditing procedure.

The most effective method to Write a Review That Sells

A definitive test for a blog audit essayist is creating a survey that is straightforward, yet at the same time changes over. At the point when done effectively, you can keep up your validity as a survey author and still create income on your blog.

Here are a few hints to enable you to draft up your next effective item audit.

Far reaching Reviews Answer Questions

An elegantly composed, fruitful item survey, should answer inquiries for your perusers:

What does this item or administration do?

What does this item do any other way than the challenge?

What does this item do is incredible?

What does this item do is awful?

Who is the perfect individual for this item?

Where would you be able to purchase this item?

As should be obvious by these precedent inquiries, you are endeavoring to answer the majority of the inquiries that a potential peruser would inquire.

At the point when a web crawler guest or standard peruser of your blog peruses this audit, they will ask themselves whether it is a smart thought to buy the item being referred to for their necessities. On the off chance that you don't answer this pertinent inquiry, they won't make a move. Your objective ought to be to reply the greatest number of inquiries as you can in the quest for giving a total item survey to your perusers.

A survey that moves leaves no stone unturned in the look for reality. As the analyst, you have to give your perusers understanding into the item or administration that they couldn't discover anyplace else. By utilizing the same number of models, pictures and video, you can convey the peruser closer to the item than any promotion spot.

Nothing Is Perfect

In your pursuit to give the most far reaching survey workable for your perusers, you have to recollect one imperative attribute of each item and administration available... NOTHING IS PERFECT.

All that you survey has both great and awful indicates that require be tended to amid the audit procedure. A typical misstep I see among bloggers is the impulse to compose celebrated promotions as audits trying to adulate different organizations into giving them free item for survey purposes.

This snare is simpler to get in than many would envision. Keep in mind... you ought to blog regarding a matter that you are energetic about, so it is normal to get amped up for getting item that you used to pay as much as possible for. Your believability is everything as an audit blogger, so it is increasingly imperative to depict reality. Your perusers will see directly past your energy on the off chance that they realize you are skirting negative parts of items trying to get all the more free stuff.

Negative surveys (and you will have some that are extremely negative after some time) ought to be reality based so you leave little contention to your decisions. You will have perusers that deviate, yet they will at any rate regard your sentiment.

Keep in mind Your Readers

When you are drafting your surveys to distribute on your blog, you have to dependably remember your regular blog peruser. On the off chance that you have been blogging for any time span, you have an entirely decent comprehension of how your perusers respond to certain dialect.

On one of my online journals regularly gotten messages and remarks about how we ought to have gotten increasingly specialized with our surveys. While there are few perusers that might want to discuss suspension bends and stun dampers, most of the perusers are either not intrigued or wouldn't comprehend the wording. Most of the perusers need to have the inquiry "will this bicycle fit my necessities?" replied, and that is the thing that we give.

Endeavor to appreciate all useful analysis and yet recollect who your normal peruser is while you compose your audits. All things considered, you need your composition to speak to your center crowd.

On the off chance that your gathering of people is a pack of web coders, it is a keen plan to get specialized. In the event that your blog perusers are searching for approaches to shed the pounds yet eat nourishment that preferences great, it's anything but a smart thought to delve into the outrageous subtleties on how sustenance is handled. Get the thought?

Abridging Features

Like it or not, there are two various types of perusers that will peruse your surveys.

The peruser that douses up each expression of your substance with the most extreme force.

The scanner that just searches for the primary concerns and takes off.

When you draft up an effective item audit, you have to make the survey work for the two sorts of blog perusers. The most straightforward approach to inspire the scanner to focus is by utilizing eye catching features all through the audit and condensing your focuses toward the finish of the article. On the off chance that you open any vehicle magazine, you can rapidly check an audit article and get fast focuses and a fundamental yes or no on the vehicle.

Toward the finish of your item and administration surveys, give a brisk synopsis passage and a rundown of the great and awful purposes of the item. This abridges the article for the in exactly the same words peruser and gives a snappy center point for the scanner.

Offshoot Links in Reviews

In the event that you composed an effective item audit, the peruser will have decided whether they have to make a move or not by the certainties you displayed. Toward the finish of your audit, embed your subsidiary connection with a strong header that obviously clarifies that the connection is for buying the item inspected. Ideally, the majority of your diligent work satisfied and your perusers that require an item like that make a move.

One final Word

Your believability as a survey essayist is everything. The more your pursue the easier it will be to accept your recommendation and have a positive involvement with the connection, the more achievement you will see with your blog and your survey composing. By no means should you ever hazard that believability for something free. When that trust is broken with your perusers, it is difficult to restore.

5 Examples of company succeeding through transparency

Straightforwardness is another objective for some, organizations, prevailing upon investors, representatives, and the overall population. At the point when a business is open about its tasks, it can procure a dimension of trust that it wouldn't have built up something else. With every year, it appears organizations are required to unveil more data, from assessment records to official pay rates.

For littler organizations, straightforwardness can be a decision. For the most part, nobody is requesting data from the vast majority of these organizations, so it's totally up to the business' heads to make data openly accessible. By being proactive in opening up its data, littler organizations can set up connections and maintain a strategic distance from the question that can happen when data is uncovered afterward. Here are five surely understood examples where organizations effectively accomplished straightforwardness.

1. Cradle - open pay rates.

Cradle made a deck that depicts the qualities that make up its way of life. The second on the rundown is "Default to straightforwardness," which the internet based life planning organization applies to every territory of its business. One way the organization has exhibited its pledge to straightforwardness is through uncovering pay rates of representatives all through the association. Through a freely accessible spreadsheet, Buffer uncovers the compensation rate of every representative by name, from prime supporter and CEO Joel Gascoigne to engineers, content crafters, and "joy saints."

Notwithstanding posting its pay rates, Buffer additionally uncovers the recipe it uses to concoct representative compensations. Every representative experiences a 45-day training camp, at that point meets all requirements for a compensation under the business' recipe, "Pay = work type X status X encounter + area (+ $10,000 if pay decision)." This sort of straightforwardness demonstrates a dimension of decency that decreases worker disappointment. At the point when representatives know the job that factors like rank and experience play in deciding pay, those workers are bound to comprehend when another representative influences a higher pay than they to do.

Related: Embrace True Transparency, and You'll Experience More Success

2. Entire Foods - GMO straightforwardness.

As a business known for offering characteristic nourishment's at greater expenses than normal supermarkets,

Whole Foods has confronted profound investigation previously. Entire Foods clients disparage the chain since they're worried about their wellbeing, so discovering that items may some way or another trade off that can be extremely unsettling to those shoppers. When Whole Foods was slapped with a legal claim blaming the chain for mislabeling items as not being results of hereditary designing, known as non-GMO, straightforwardness turned into a need for the organization.

Right now, Whole Foods is chipping away at turning into the primary national basic need fasten to offer full GMO straightforwardness with its undertakings. With an objective of 2018 for full organization, the task will require each item sold as non-GMO to experience a check procedure. The organization has constantly urged its providers to put its items through a confirmation procedure, also. Entire Foods trusts that by making this promise to GMO straightforwardness, it will empower industry-wide straightforwardness, with makers and merchants making the inquiries that should be inquired.

Related: 4 Ways to Instill and Promote Transparency in a Workplace

3. Zappos - visits and merchant get to

Straightforwardness is composed specifically into the Zappos Family Core Values, in the announcement, "Construct Open and Honest Relationships With Communication." This is exemplified by a whole division in the association called Zappos Insights, which encourages voyages through the Zappos home office and live preparing occasions. Participants can even calendar Q&A sessions with explicit offices inside Zappos, including client benefit, client experience, and showcasing.

Maybe the most quick explanation about Zappos' responsibility straightforwardness originated from CEO Tony Hsieh in his book Delivering Happiness: A Path to Profits, Passion, and Purpose. In the book, Hsieh discloses his choice to open up access to data to the organization's merchants. Beforehand, organizations had constantly kept sellers in obscurity, feeling that they expected to nearly monitor their mysteries. Because of his thought, Zappos made an extranet that gives merchants finish perceivability into their business.

Related: Let's Be Real: Why Transparency in Business Should Be the Norm

4. SumAll - pay straightforwardness.

Like Buffer, SumAll chose to open up data about its pay rates yet it did as such from its first days in business. The organization offers compensation data in a Google Doc that is available to each worker in the association. Thus, the organization says it has a diminished turnover rate since when representatives are discontent with their pay rates, they don't hesitate to talk up about their disappointment. For SumAll, straightforwardness implies ensuring each worker recognizes what's happening all through the association consistently.

On its site, SumAll nitty gritty the apparatuses it uses to accomplish wanted straightforwardness levels.

Representatives use work the executives programming, texting, Google Drive, and up close and personal correspondence to ensure everybody realizes what's happening outside of their own groups. An organization Wiki holds the majority of SumAll's strategy data, including the organization's basic beliefs and data about the corporate culture.

5. Patagonia - store network straightforwardness.

For outwear organization Patagonia, giving straightforwardness all through its store network implies diminishing any negative social and ecological effects the organization may have. While numerous organizations have been found napping by data about ecologically antagonistic propensities for its makers or wholesalers. To maintain a strategic distance from this, Patagonia adopts a proactive strategy, assuming the liability on itself to ensure no mischief is being caused really taking shape of its items. The task is designated "Impression Chronicles" and is shown to the overall population through recordings on the organization's site.

At the point when a client taps on a thing on the Patagonia site, that client approaches a progression of Footprint Chronicles recordings straightforwardly identified with that item. These recordings demonstrate each progression of the store network, including every single material plant and sewing manufacturing plants utilized in making the thing. From that page, clients can click over to the fundamental Footprint Chronicles page to see the organization's general store network. On the off chance that a piece of the assembling procedure should be enhanced, Patagonia lets it out straightforwardly in the video and welcomes input from clients by they way it can move forward.

At the point when organizations are unguarded with workers, investors, and the overall population, those organizations can assemble trust while likewise considering themselves responsible. Organizations of all sizes can utilize these equivalent standards to enhance their own inward procedures, which will enhance both representative assurance and consumer loyalty.

5 Examples of customer experience innovation

Serena Williams is a savagely aggressive tennis player. Her record is 39 Grand Slam titles. She demonstrates a capacity to serve experts at basic minutes — a tennis serve the rival can't make contact with. She's known for her forceful play, a "high hazard" style adjusted to a limited extent by her serve, the best in ladies' tennis history. She reliably puts incredible shots with precision. She isn't thrown off by variety of conditions. She won the Australian open while two months pregnant. On the off chance that you've at any point been pregnant, you know going for a long walk pregnant is hard. However, Serena was not going to withdraw, even in her most powerless minute.

The best competitors on the planet go out on a limb in basic minutes. Serena is an incredible notice of how to be a pioneer in indeterminate occasions. Like Serena's playing style, organizations today should reliably make strong wagers on client encounter even in questionable occasions.

One territory we have to complete a superior occupation of hazard taking is client encounter. Ongoing exploration demonstrates that last year 75% of organizations said their best goal for the year was enhancing client encounter. In any case, how do organizations realize how to do that? There is a noteworthy job for advancement with regards to enhanced client encounters.

Writer Michael Docherty writes in his book Collective Disruption: How Corporations and Startups Can Co-Create Transformative New Businesses about Growth Horizons, a McKinsey structure that separates the rates with regards to dealing with the center business versus development. The Growth Horizon informs pioneers go through 70% with respect to their time on shielding the organizations' center. These are the standard items and administrations that the organization wound up fruitful moving. Next 20% of time and assets ought to be spent on extending those present items and administrations. Finally, 10% of time and assets must be spent on transformative development. Transformative development is the advancement that movements or turns an organization's whole system. Most organizations don't invest enough energy in transformative development since they aren't great at transformative and it's frightening for them. A model is Amazon that moves into another industry medium-term. We've seen numerous instances of this by Amazon including the ongoing securing of Whole Foods Market.

We are at a point where organizations need to forcefully advance their client encounter. The organizations that do this will eventually win more piece of the pie. There is an enormous expanding opportunity with regards to client encounter in light of the fact that most organizations are basically horrible at it. In any case, these ventures would expect organizations to make intense moves in dubious occasions. Today it is too simple to even consider being imitated, to be ripped off — for brands not to proceed to develop and move the needle with transformative development.

It's useful for you to consider ways you can develop the client encounter, taking a gander at organizations that have really done it. Here are five different ways you can develop your client encounter gaining from organizations Lemonade, McDonalds, Amazon, Walmart, and one useful example.

Wed Efficiency With Giving Back

One case of an industry ready for interruption is the protection business. Most clients are mistaken and baffled for insurance agencies. A client must pay a lofty month to month expense to a protection supplier, and when that client needs inclusion, the insurance agency regularly treats the client ineffectively. Most clients purchase protection with the learning that they will get little an incentive out of relationship. Protection client ventures are conceivably the most exceedingly awful out of any industry.

The client venture needs a refresh. Cases are handled in the manner in which that they generally have been. Numerous workers still touch the case. Regularly insurance agencies expect clients to send in case data through the mail. You can't generally record a case on the web and infrequently on your telephone. However, one start-up set out to change all that. Daniel Schreiber, fellow benefactor of new insurance agency Lemonade said in a meeting, "Protection is broadly considered an 'essential underhandedness." Lemonade has changed the plan of action. Lemonade removes a settled charge from the client's regularly scheduled installments, pays reinsurance (and some unavoidable costs) and uses the rest for paying out cases. Their client ventures are versatile agreeable. It doesn't take long to get a reaction in regards to a case. Lemonade, utilizing man-made reasoning has made the endorsing and claims process less demanding. The subsequent client encounter turns out to be increasingly consistent, prompt and dependable. As per Lemonade, 87% of their clients are first time protection purchasers. Lemonade requests to an underserved showcase. Twenty to thirty year olds love the amazing way with Lemonade, any unclaimed protection cash will be given to a philanthropy of the client's decision. They've effectively hitched proficiency with cognizant free enterprise in an industry that numerous clients don't trust.

Give Customers Tools To Do Things Themselves

McDonalds was the first eatery network to concentrate on operational proficiency and benefits. Everything about its DNA was centered around these things. While they sold the possibility of "network" and "family esteems," when you find out about the starting point story, it was around one man's drive to profit (Ray Kroc). McDonalds as of late taken off clerk booths so clients don't collaborate with an individual while paying for their nourishment. While some have financial feelings of dread that robots will supplant individuals, numerous clients and corporate pioneers incline toward effectiveness and speed of mechanization. Will we see more organizations deciding on computerization? Or then again organizations taking a hard position against robotization to construct a people first affair? I think man-made brainpower loans itself pleasantly to cheap food - in light of the fact that these clients are there on the grounds that they need quick encounters. You would not discover this involvement with a semi-formal eatery with nearby create. There are some decent parts of having individuals, for example, the human touch, the instruction about the items or administrations, and the dramatic artistry of the experience. While giving clients devices to do things themselves doesn't constantly mean installment stands, McDonalds realizes its client base. Its clients need quick administration. On the off chance that you give them proficient devices so they can do things themselves, it may be a success win for you and your clients.

Accelerate And Simplify Retail Interactions

The most tedious piece of shopping in a retail location is swimming through stuff that is not significant for you — the client. For instance I adore the investment funds I get from top of the line rebate stores however to get those reserve funds in the store I need to burrow through huge amounts of stuff that I don't care for or need. Before the finish of the shopping trip I am worn out. The investment funds I get includes some major disadvantages. What happens when an organization will have the capacity to remove the work for the client and give focused valuing? Walmart is trying mammoth stands in their stores, called "pickup towers." To utilize the pinnacle, clients check a scanner tag on their buy receipt. Inside 45 seconds, an entryway on the machine opens, and the things show up on a transport line. This spares the client time, yet enables them to get their things - along these lines they don't need to stress over bundles being stolen for the duration of the day.

Grasp Transparency — Don't Coerce Or Confuse Customers

As of late I got an email from Groupon that there was some peculiar conduct with my record. I don't utilize Groupon and I went to erase my record today. Prepare to be blown away. It's difficult to erase your record yourself. I invested energy everywhere throughout the site, in the assistance segment, and after that on Google. No erase account that is anything but difficult to discover! At the point when organizations make it so difficult to erase your record, it makes me think they need high numbers to tell their board "look what number of clients we have!" However on the off chance that the clients are individuals like me who never again get an incentive out of the administration, is that an important organization? To what extent will they drag individuals alongside their quantities of inert clients. For what reason don't they make it less demanding for clients to erase their record? Groupon is a case of an organization that utilizes guile in their client adventure to blow up their numbers. In any case, what organization has flourished by deceiving their clients? On the off chance that a client needs to erase their record, make it simple for them to do as such. You are possibly deceiving your load up individuals in the event that you have a great many latent clients since you made it unthinkable for them to leave. Give genuine incentive to individuals and they will remain. Be that as it may, don't deceive them into staying stayed with you. You can withdraw, however I need my record completely erased from the site. Make it simple for the client!

Trust Customers To Test Your Products Before Buying Them

Amazon is propelling a Try Before You Buy Service. This is colossal for retail. In what capacity will the other membership based retailers contend with that? Fundamentally every online retailer ought to be concerned. That is the primary torment with organizations like Nordstrom Rack, where when you purchase a thing and return it, it costs you, the client, in excess of 5 bucks. For somebody like me who purchases stuff all the time on the web and needs to trade an alternate size, that is an issue — and a great deal of cash. Amazon again is making client's lives essentially less demanding and better — and they will keep on picking up piece of the overall industry in doing that.

What are the manners in which you can improve clients lives less demanding and? In the event that you begin from that point you will end up with huge amounts of incredible thoughts, and your business will go from upset to disruptor.

10 easy ways to get Customers to write reviews Boost Sales!

1. Ask, ask, inquire. It's the most clear one, however you should ensure both yourself and your staff are approaching clients for their input at whatever point conceivable. 70% of clients are glad to leave an audit when inquired.

2. Counter Display or pop-up. An extremely simple route is to put out a pop-up, similar to a tent card, that requests that your guests survey. Indeed, even a sticker on your front entryway referencing that you're on Foursquare, TripAdvisor or Yelp can remind individuals to check in or leave an audit.

3. Email. In the event that you have your clients' email addresses, it's a little

exertion to send them an email update a couple of days after their underlying buy or visit with you, requesting that they leave an audit. You can even robotize this procedure with instruments, for example, Square Marketing.

4. Customer Survey. Each business needs to manage questions, concerns or issues. After you or your client benefit staff settle an issue, inquire as to whether the client needs to audit your business on Google or Yelp and so on. When you make this a piece of your client benefit process you will without a doubt see an expansion in audits for your business.

5. Client survey Solution. There are a few programming devices available that have practical experience in client communication and online audit the board. A standout amongst the most famous one being Podium. Others incorporate Review-Trackers and Real Time Reviews.

6. Incentive. You must be extremely careful about paying your clients for audits on the grounds that most survey locales dishearten that and may even

punish your posting when they discover you've been paying clients for surveys. Yet, offering a little motivating force, for example, a free beverage or treat upon their following visit to your bistro, for instance, is consummately fine and an extremely powerful approach to create more surveys for your business.

7. Social Media. Consider asking your fans or devotees on Facebook and Twitter to survey your business once every while. You should open yourself up to analysis from individuals yet it could be a successful method to develop a volume of audits.

8. Send a postcard! Truly, you read that right. There are numerous ways you can approach your clients for some help that take less time and are more affordable, yet none of them can very match the adequacy of sending a customized postcard trough snail mail.

9. Update on solicitations. What about putting a sentence or two on each receipt you conveyed, requesting that your customers survey your organization on their favored site. For computerized

solicitations, you can even incorporate connections.

10. Send a push message: on the off chance that you have officially faithful clients enlisted on an advanced faithfulness card, for example, Loopy Loyalty you can convey a pop-up message specifically to their cell phone after they have visited your store, asking them pleasantly to leave a survey. You can even offer them a little motivating force to do as such, for example, two or three stamps towards their next remuneration.

www.ingramcontent.com/pod-product-compliance
Lightning Source LLC
Chambersburg PA
CBHW071215220526
45468CB00002B/618